MAKING COMMON SENSE

Leadership as Meaning-making
in a Community of Practice

MAKING COMMON SENSE

Leadership as Meaning-making in a Community of Practice

Wilfred H. Drath and Charles J. Palus

Center for Creative Leadership
Greensboro, North Carolina

The Center for Creative Leadership is an international, nonprofit educational institution founded in 1970 to advance the understanding, practice, and development of leadership for the benefit of society worldwide. As a part of this mission, it publishes books and reports that aim to contribute to a general process of inquiry and understanding in which ideas related to leadership are raised, exchanged, and evaluated. The ideas presented in its publications are those of the author or authors.

The Center thanks you for supporting its work through the purchase of this volume. If you have comments, suggestions, or questions about any Center publication, please contact John R. Alexander, President, at the address given below.

Center for Creative Leadership
Post Office Box 26300
Greensboro, North Carolina 27438-6300

©1994 Center for Creative Leadership

All rights reserved. No part of this publication may be reproduced, stored in a retrieval system, or transmitted, in any form or by any means, electronic, mechanical, photocopying, recording, or otherwise, without the prior written permission of the publisher. Printed in the United States of America.

CCL No. 156

Library of Congress Cataloging-in-Publication Data

Drath, Wilfred H.
    Making common sense: leadership as meaning-making in a community of practice / Wilfred H. Drath and Charles J. Palus
       p. cm
    Includes bibliographical references.
    ISBN 0-912879-97-1
    1. Leadership.   I. Palus, Charles J. II. Title.
    HD57.7.D735   1994
    658.4'092—dc20   94-17583
                                                                                          CIP

Table of Contents

Acknowledgments vii

Preface ix

Introduction 1
    The Importance of Making Meaning 2
    Applying Meaning to Leadership 4

Discussion of Terms 7
    Meaning 7
    Meaning-making 9
    Community of Practice 11

People in Positions of Authority:
A New View of Five Concepts 13
    From Social Influence to Social Meaning-making 14
    From a Dominant Individual Leader Acting on Followers to People
        Participating in a Shared Process 14
    From Motivation to Act to Frameworks Within Which to Act 17
    From the Authority Figure as De Facto Leader to the Authority Figure as a
        Participant in a Process of Leadership 18
    From "How Do I Take Charge and Make Things Happen?" to "How Do I
        Participate in an Effective Process of Leadership?" 19

Implications: So What Is Leadership Development? 21

Conclusion: Changing Constructs of Leadership 23

Bibliography 26

Acknowledgments

This essay is in a true sense the result of a collaborative effort involving friends and colleagues we have talked and argued with over the last two years. All of these people have participated in a vigorous process of shaping our ideas. Of course, helping to shape does not necessarily imply agreement, and only the authors are responsible for the final form the ideas are in. We are deeply grateful for everyone's participation and support.

Constructive criticism from our colleagues was invaluable. The following people provided us with thoughtful reviews of early or later drafts: Jack Bowen, Doug Bowie, Robert Burkhart, Bob Burnside, Nancy Dixon, Diane Ducat, Dal Fisher, Per Grøholt, Barry Gruenberg, Stan Gryskiewicz, Dave Hills, Michael Hoppe, Owen Jacobs, Lily Kelly, Winn Legerton, Mike Malone, Pam Mayer, Cindy McCauley, Glenn Mehltretter, Peter Neary, Sharon Rogolsky, Marian Ruderman, Sara Schley, Lanty Smith, William Torbert, Walt Tornow, Cresencio Torres, Walt Ulmer, and Ellen Van Velsor. To each of them we say thank you.

We would also like to thank our editor, Martin Wilcox, for his masterful tightening and clarifying of what was a rather sloshing manuscript. The loose conceptual cannons that remain are, alas, our own.

Preface

Several years ago at the Center for Creative Leadership, we began considering whether the Center should endorse and disseminate a definition of leadership. Meetings were held, the staff was asked to submit definitions, an extensive literature review was conducted, and a survey of our colleagues, both practitioners and researchers, was taken to find out how they define leadership. A surprising number of definitions was submitted.

What was even more surprising to us when we looked at them was how, despite differences in emphases, they all seemed to be the product of a single perspective—or perhaps two very similar perspectives. As we read them we found ourselves having the same feeling over and over: Something was missing. It was not that they were wrong; rather that something important was not being accounted for.

This feeling was not entirely new to us. We have often felt something like it when we took part in the Center's action-research (which combines studying executives with assisting them in their professional development). Even after executives have received feedback from various evaluations, they may still ask, "What is it that I need to do in order to become a better leader?" The instruments that are available today and the concepts that underlie them also seem to come from one perspective.

Thus, we began work on this paper. The Center ultimately decided not to adopt any single definition (because the range of its activities, from training to research, makes it impractical to have just one). Similarly, in writing this paper, we have decided not to try to define leadership. Rather, we are trying to develop a different way of looking at it.

We invite you to join us in taking a vantage point on leadership that we think is promising. In doing this, we do not mean to imply that your notion of leadership is naive or otherwise thoughtless; in fact, just the opposite. We assume that you have in the course of your life fashioned a working understanding of it that allows you to participate with others in various kinds of cooperative social undertakings. We don't just *want* to leave your working understanding intact; we *must* leave it intact because without it you could not evaluate or make use of what we're saying.

This paper, then, will involve you in taking a look at your notion of leadership in light of our notion. It will involve you in testing our viewpoint against your experiences with people who are called *leaders* and groups that operate with leadership.

We would like to emphasize that this paper is part of work in progress. We would like to have more good examples, but good examples are hard-won through taking ideas into experience and seeing if they can explain what's happening. That is the next step for us.

If you bear with us, however, we hope that reading this paper will be worth your while. If you are a manager, it may give you a glimpse of how people can get better at working together to solve hard problems, a more useful notion of what we can expect from individuals in positions of authority, and a wider appreciation for the role of leadership in our lives. If you are a researcher who works with the concept of leadership, it may stimulate you to use perspectives other than influence and provide a way of thinking about leadership that is consonant with the constructive-developmental orientation and with the work being done on organizational learning from the community-of-practice angle.

Introduction

Suppose you have been given the assignment of forming a new unit within a corporation. The unit—which is ongoing, not a task force—is responsible for designing, assisting in the implementation of, and monitoring the corporation's "green" practices. You have been assigned people from a variety of functions, but everyone has some interest in, and detailed knowledge of, environmental issues. As the nominal leader of this new unit, imagine your first meeting.

Everyone is talking, trying to get air time. Feeling a responsibility to make the time productive, you try to bring a degree of order to this by flip-charting some agenda items, structuring people's participation, and so forth. This is only partly effective. The meeting ends on a somewhat confused and dissatisfied note. The main questions seem to be, What is it we are trying to do and how are we going to do it? There is no general agreement about the answers.

You return to your office and ponder the situation. You take your responsibility seriously; you want to be effective as the leader of this new unit. What are the key questions you ask yourself at this moment?

More than likely, they are something like these:

(1) How can I take charge of this group of headstrong and knowledgeable people?

(2) How can I influence these people to work together harmoniously?

(3) How can I make them accept my influence willingly, so that I don't have to act in an authoritarian way? (Because I know that won't work with this group!)

(4) How can I make good things happen in this group and discharge the responsibility I've been given?

(5) In short, how can I exercise effective leadership?

These are not bad questions, but we don't think that they will help you deal effectively and directly with all the issues and situations that the group will face. We think the questions have a limited utility because they all derive from one perspective on leadership—one that sees leadership in terms of dominance and influence: It assumes leadership is happening when an individual called a *leader* acts in some way to change the behavior or attitudes of others called *followers*.

If you want to ask additional questions that will help you with this group, we think you need to take a different perspective on leadership. In this paper we will suggest that you look at leadership as a social meaning-making process that occurs in groups of people who are engaged in some activity together.

If you return to your office to ponder the situation while holding this second view of leadership, you would be likely to ask yourself questions such as:

(1) What is the nature of this group of people? Do we have any history of working together?

(2) What is the most effective process of leadership for this group at this time? How might that process change as the group develops into a community with shared history?

(3) How can I, as a holder of some authority derived from being named as chairperson, participate productively in this process of leadership?

We believe that these questions are significantly different from the first set and can lead to importantly different behaviors on the part of any person endowed with authority in a group, as well as on the parts of people in the group with less authority. We also believe that many of the challenges faced by people in organizations today call for new ways of understanding leadership—what it is and what it can and cannot do. We hope to offer here some useful ideas for rethinking leadership, leadership development, and leadership theory. We also hope, in spite of the abstract nature of our inquiry, to be able to say, before the end of this paper, something of practical value to people in positions of authority who would participate in effective processes of leadership. Before that, however, we must back up and start at the beginning. The beginning is the need for people to make sense of their experience.

The Importance of Making Meaning

Whatever else we can say about people, one thing that we all share—across cultures, geography, and time—is the ability, and the hunger, to make things make sense. What does "making sense" mean? This is a hard question that has been dealt with historically in the writings of Wittgenstein, Berkeley, and Kant, to name only three. Our work has been guided mostly by the writings of Nelson Goodman (1978), Jerome Bruner (1986), and Robert Kegan (1982). In the interest of brevity, let's say that making sense is the process of arranging our understanding of experience so that we can know what has happened and what is happening, and so that we can predict what will happen; it is constructing knowledge of ourself and the world.

This is not the only way of talking about making sense. We could say that making sense is the process of discovering what is really happening. Many, perhaps most, prefer to view reality in this way—as something that can be more or less directly known. It is not our purpose here to refute such a view. Rather, we invite you to consider another view and see what it suggests about leadership. Let's assume that there is no way to determine what is ultimately real, that the best we can hope for is to make arrangements in our minds that create a coherence out of our experience. This view is called *constructivism* (Bruner, 1986; Fingarette, 1963; Goodman, 1984; Kegan, 1982; Piaget, 1954).

Taking the constructivist perspective, consider the following example of the process of understanding. You are out for a walk and the sky grows dark and you hear a distant rumbling sound. Unless you have a peculiar phobia, you do not panic and cower in fear. You know what is happening. But how have you come to know this? How have you come to possess a set of assumptions about what you are hearing? How are you able to interpret the sights and sounds so that you know what they mean and, more, so that you can anticipate and plan your actions accordingly?

One answer is that you have constructed this knowledge out of the raw material of your experience, which of course includes being told about thunderstorms by others from the time of your earliest memories. This construction of the experience of a thunderstorm constitutes your understanding and therefore makes up the reality of such storms for you. Let's give a name to that set of assumptions in your head that allows you to interpret sensory information, anticipate future events, and plan accordingly. Let's call it a *meaning-making structure*. Understanding can then be said to consist of a process of using meaning-making structures to construct knowledge about experience so that one is able to interpret, anticipate, and plan. Meaning-making makes sense of an action by placing it within some larger frame, and this frame is seen by the person who makes sense as the way the world is and thus guides the person in his or her way of being in the world (Bruner, 1986; Goodman, 1978). In this way, reality is said to be a construction.

In this constructivist view, people make meaning individually—they construct their own personal experience so that it makes sense for various periods in their lives as they grow and develop (Kegan, 1982; Kelly, 1955; Perry, 1968)—and people make meaning socially—they construct their experience together (Berger & Luckman, 1966; Bruner, 1986; Goodman, 1978) so that they can communicate and cooperate and agree about what is happening. They can interpret, anticipate, and plan together. The processes of individual meaning-making and social meaning-making are deeply interrelated, as individuals are deeply related to the social systems in which they live.

What are the implications of this for leadership?

Applying Meaning to Leadership

Adopting the constructivist view, we can see leadership as a tool that people use in their relations with one another. The purpose of this tool is to make sense, to make meaning. Leadership in organizations can likewise be seen as more about making meaning than about making decisions and influencing people. The process of making meaning in certain kinds of social settings constitutes leadership. In other words, we can regard leadership as meaning-making in a community of practice.

There are other processes of meaning-making, to be sure. For individuals, there are such processes as learning, ego development, and spiritual development. In social contexts, there are such processes as language, knowledge systems, the arts, and, of course, on the largest scale, culture itself. Leadership, as a type of social meaning-making process, is related to other such processes but discernibly different from them by virtue of its application in a community of practice (that is, a group of people with a shared history of doing something, usually work, together).

There are other ways to express this idea. The words we use in this paper seem to be the shortest way to say it, and that's why we like them, but it is not necessary to use just those words. One might just as well say that leadership is the process of making sense of what people are doing together so that people will understand and be committed. Or one might say that leadership is the social sense-making process that creates interpersonal influence—in other words, one person does what some other person influences him or her to do because doing it makes sense to both people. We hope you will be able to think of other ways of expressing the idea as we go along. Putting the idea in different words is a way of exploring it.

Still another way to talk about this is to lay out the terms we use, define them briefly, and then try to string them together. *Meaning* can be thought of as a cognitive and emotional framework (an internal structure of ideas and feelings) that allows a person to know (in the sense of understand) some *world version* (a representation of the way things are and the way they ought to be) and that places the person in relation to this world version. Given this way of thinking about meaning, *meaning-making* then consists of the creation, nurturance, and evolution (or revolution) of these cognitive and emotional frameworks. When the making of such frameworks happens in a *community of practice* (people united in a common enterprise who share a history and thus certain values, beliefs, ways of talking, and ways of doing things), then we can say that leadership is happening.

To repeat, we are not offering this as a definition of leadership. With definitions, people rightly call on the definer to defend the truth, or at least the internal consistency, of the definition. We would prefer you regard our outlook *as if* it were true and see where that might lead. What we are offering is a way of categorizing, or a scheme of organizing, the concept of leadership. As Nelson Goodman (1978, p. 129) points out, the argument in support of such an offering consists not of defending the truth of the scheme but rather of arguing for its efficacy in understanding leadership as a concept and phenomenon. Thus, you need not give up your own definition of leadership. Better, in fact, to hang onto it and to experiment with viewing your own understanding of leadership in light of the outlook being offered here.

How is this view of leadership significantly different from other views? What do we see as the major advantages of adopting this view?

At the highest level of abstraction, what is different about the view offered here is that most other views begin with the assumption that leadership is a dominance-cum-social-influence process. Most existing theories, models, and definitions of leadership proceed from the assumption that somehow leadership is about getting people to do something. In our view, dominance is but one approach to meaning-making (though perhaps, in complex situations, not often the best approach), and social influence is another approach and can also be seen as an outcome of leadership, but not the only outcome (problem solving, satisfaction, actualization, closure, and significance are some others, for example) and it is not the only reason humans engage in leadership.

The difference in these two basic views rests on deep assumptions about the nature of human energy and motivation. The dominance-cum-social-influence view assumes that humans are naturally still, at rest, and that they need some motivating force to get them going. The meaning-making view being offered here, on the other hand, assumes that people are naturally in motion, always doing something (Kelly, 1955), and that they need, rather than motivation to act, frameworks within which their actions make sense.

Out of this major difference in underlying assumption arises another important difference and, we think, an important advantage: When you do not see dominance and social influence as the basic activities of leadership, you no longer need to think of leadership predominantly in terms of leaders (people who influence others) and followers (those who are influenced). Instead, you can think about leadership as a process in which everyone in a community, or group, is engaged. This is a way of viewing leadership as part of a context. Leadership, instead of being a generic force that a person called a *leader* can apply willy-nilly to any group of people, becomes a community-specific process that arises in various forms and with various effects whenever people attempt to work together. People may play varying roles, some involving formal authority and power, which may offer the opportunity to make unique contributions to the process of leadership, but we need not extend special status to these roles above others, as all roles can be seen as contributing uniquely. This means that we may be able to disentangle power and authority from leadership (Heifetz, in press) and this in turn may allow us to better understand the relationship of these various social processes (power, authority, leadership) to one another.

This last point bears repeating and emphasis. In the view of leadership being offered here, authority, which Heifetz (in press) defines as "conferred power to perform a service," is quite different from leadership. Being related, the two phenomena are, we think, often confused, and this confuses much of the thinking about both authority and leadership. In the terms we offer here, authority is an important means of generating coherence within groups, organizations, and societies and is thus a frequent tool by which meaning is made in communities of practice; it, therefore, is often used in the leadership process. But to confuse authority and leadership is to confuse means and ends. Authority is a tool for making sense of things (making meaning) but so are other human tools such as norms, values, work systems, and goal-path structures. Leadership, on the other hand, is understood here as the *process* through which people put these tools to work to create meaning.

Taking this view of leadership may also allow us to add to our concepts of leadership development (see Palus & Drath, in press). Instead of focusing leadership development almost exclusively on training individuals to be leaders, we may, using this view, learn to develop leadership by improving everyone's ability to participate in the process of leadership. This would require research to help us understand what roles, behaviors, and capacities are involved in leadership as a social meaning-making process.

By allowing us to better see leadership as a shared human process, as an activity that people engage in together, seeing leadership as meaning-making may also help us clarify the relationship between certain individual traits (such as intelligence, dominance, initiative-taking, and risk-taking) and leadership. We may come to see that the people we call *natural leaders* (charismatic leaders, powerful individual leaders, inspired leaders) are the people who are able, for reasons of intelligence, knowledge, and experience, to express formulations of meaning in behalf of a community—they can say what people have in their minds and hearts—and that doing this often seems to imbue these people with almost superhuman characteristics, and that these characteristics can then subsequently be difficult to disentangle from the process of leadership. We may be surprised to learn just how social this process we see as individual leadership really is. We may also come to see that the leadership process is not limited to individuals making meaning in behalf of the community. Other, more distributed processes may thus become available to people to improve their life and work together.

Discussion of Terms

In this section, we take an in-depth look at the words that we use to express this view of leadership.

Meaning

Meaning is an elusive word. In this paper we are not trying to use it in a philosophical sense, only in a practical sense. We are aiming to reflect what people seem to generally agree they mean when they use it.

Basically speaking, *meaning* has two broad senses in common usage (Fingarette, 1963). The first has to do with the way words and other symbols stand for, refer to, or represent phenomena (or other words or symbols). The second sense involves people's values and relationships and commitments. In our rough-and-ready working sense of *meaning* as it applies to leadership, we will use both, but it will be useful to approach each as a separate case at first.

The first sense of *meaning*—that of how words and other symbols stand for things—rather obviously comes into play when people use language with one another. In this paper we will be interested in some special ways of using language: specifically, naming and interpreting.

Naming may seem rather unimportant to leadership at first. But putting a name to something is more than a way of pointing at it; it is also a way of saying that it exists. Naming something categorizes it, which puts it into a certain context and relationship to other things. A name confers membership in a class of things that already exists, emphasizes certain characteristics while looking past others, and allows comparison and differentiation. Because of the power of language to shape our very understanding of what is real, these contexts and memberships in categories bring things into existence for us. An example of how this works is when Thoreau called a certain kind of crime *civil disobedience*. Suddenly it was possible for some people to do things they would not have done before. Names can carry with them whole ways of being in the world.

Naming and putting things into categories leads naturally to interpretation. Interpretation plays an important role in leadership (Pondy, 1978; Smircich & Morgan, 1982.) It can be understood as the act of explaining what things are, why they have happened or are about to happen, and what can and should be done as a result. Interpretation depends upon an underlying worldview that is in turn built up of a vastly complex interweaving of names and classifications. The meaning of an event or a thing depends upon the names (and subsequent classifications) one gives to the elements of the event or thing. Examples of this are almost too easy to think of. Is the faltering economy a threat or an opportunity? Or is the economy faltering at all? Are we in the computer business or the information-processing business? Are we overdelegating work to subordinates or are we empowering them to think for themselves?

The first sense of meaning, then, is this sense of words and other symbols standing for ideas, phenomena, and other symbols and providing a context of understanding and interpreting the world, of making the world make sense. The second sense of meaning that we will be using in talking about leadership as meaning-making involves people and their values and commitments.

Margaret Farley (1986) writes, "The history of the human race, as well as the story of any one life, might be told in terms of commitments." (p. 12). This is the aspect of meaning most commonly being addressed when people express a need to feel that work, or a relationship, or life, is meaningful. People do things or take part in things and thus commit to things that they see as being important, not trivial; valuable, not worthless. People make commitments to other people, to ideas, to values, to goals, and to missions. More subtly, people make commitments to the kinds of meaning we have already discussed, to ways of naming and thinking about things, to ways of being in the world, ways of understanding the world, oneself, and one's place in the world (Fingarette, 1963; Kegan, 1982; Kelly, 1955). The process of leadership can involve any or all of these kinds of commitments. In an organization, for example, we make commitments to goals, of course, but also to other people and to ideas and to values.

In thinking about meaning as the basis of leadership, we will think of both of these aspects of meaning—the aspect of naming and categorizing, and thus interpreting, and the aspect of believing and valuing, and thus committing. Being a member of The Clean Parks Club, for example, may be meaningful because (1) we can name ourselves as part of the group; we belong and the membership partly defines who we are. And such membership can further be meaningful because (2) we put ourselves into a committed relationship with others in the group; we sign on to play some role (vice-president or task-force chairperson or worker bee), and this role implies commitments and relationships to others. Finally, we make a commitment through this membership to the wider community and we can assign value or importance to that. Both of these aspects of meaning are thus being addressed when someone says, "As vice-president of The Clean Parks Club, I helped make our town a better place to live."

Meaning-making

If meaning can be thought of as naming, interpreting, and making commitments to actions, to other people, and to values, then meaning-making is the process of creating names, interpretations, and commitments. Meaning-making is all about constructing a sense of what is, what actually exists, and, of that, what is important. People can and do construct a sense of what is and what is important for themselves; people also construct with others, together, a socially oriented sense of what is and what is important. When this happens in association with practice (work, activity) in a community, we say that the process of leadership is happening.

A key issue here is how private, personal meaning-making is connected to public, social meaning-making. Let's go back to our crime/civil disobedience example. You could, if you wished, make a private classification of what is generally considered a crime—say, spray-painting cars—as a prank. No one would stop you from coming up with any number of classification schemes different from socially agreed upon schemes. But what meaning would such schemes have? They would face difficulty as interpretive tools, for only you would understand how to apply them to the object or event being interpreted. Such private schemes would also face difficulty in creating commitments—people resist committing to things they do not understand.

This is an issue that, for example, artists face every day: How does one transform a private meaning into a public meaning? The writer may have names for events and feelings, ways of thinking and talking about commitments and values, that only he or she understands. To make his or her way of understanding the world useful to others the writer must make meaning; get outside of himself or herself and find words, metaphors, plots, characters, images, and so forth that open up private names and values to the minds and hearts of others. It is in this sense of reaching out beyond the self that the artist is said to communicate his or her vision. (Doing so, by the way, can be seen as being part of a process of leadership within a community of practice we call the arts.)

This is what people in positions of authority must also try to do if they would participate in an effective process of leadership. At the end of World War II, one of his generals remarked to Winston Churchill that his stirring speeches throughout the war had inspired the English people and had been in large measure responsible for victory. Churchill replied that he had only said what was already in people's hearts. His speeches inspired people partly because his words represented to them their own commitments and values. This was part of what they, as a culturally united people, shared. Yet, Churchill was also making meaning in behalf of a community of practice we might call *English people at war with*

Hitler. He was not only reflecting meanings that were already present; he was connecting meanings to one another in new ways appropriate to the unique demands of the situation. It is interesting to think about what in his life and character had prepared him to do this—to create a framework for interpretation and understanding in behalf of an entire nation—but more, what in the life of that community of practice made it possible. In another time and another context, Winston Churchill might have been a minor bureaucrat or a failed artist.

Meaning-making is in many respects an individual activity, but it is also necessarily social and collective. As individuals, we are all embedded in cultures; from these cultures we start out life with certain characteristic ways of understanding the world that are given (Goodman, 1978). In making meaning within our own heads and in our experience with others, we draw on a common book of given ways of knowing—these constitute our culture.

From this viewpoint, the most general tool for meaning-making in a society is culture. Culture is a kind of grandparent of all leadership (see Schein, 1992). Thus, processes of leadership are connected to the larger cultural frame within which they occur—culture-building is the primary process of meaning-making in collective experience and thus the primary leadership process. Culture provides people with givens in the form of names for things, ways of classifying and thus interpreting things. And culture also provides the basic givens that guide our relationships and commitments and our sense of lasting value.

More specifically, meaning-making happens through such processes as identifying vision and mission, framing problems, setting goals, arguing and engaging in dialogue, theory-building and -testing, storytelling, and the making of contracts and agreements. To some extent or another, all of these meaning-making processes happen in hierarchical organizations. It is worth repeating that these process are not merely important to leadership, rather they constitute leadership.

In the view of leadership being offered here, this is an important distinction. Often, there is a tendency to think about meaning as something that happens as a result of leadership. This might be put, as Warren Bennis (1991) did, "A leader creates meaning. You start with vision. You build trust. And you create meaning." The distinction that seems important to us is that, instead of being a behavior that leaders may or may not engage in, meaning-making constitutes, makes up, leadership. From an individual perspective, it's not so much that a person is first a leader and then creates meaning; it's more that, in making meaning (and remember, we understand "making" to include the creation, nurturance, and evolution of meaning), a person comes to be called a leader. In addition, making meaning is not an activity that is limited to a process in which an individual manages meaning for everyone else. People can make meaning in a collective sense, and that is leadership as well. It is the process of participating in making meaning in a collective sense that makes leaders out of people.

Community of Practice

Community of practice refers to an idea that is different from, although related to, the idea of group, team, collective, aggregate, and so forth. The key word is *practice*, and the key difference lies in the power of shared activity to create shared knowledge and shared ways of knowing. In a community of practice, people are united by more than membership in a group or category, they are involved with one another in action (Lave & Wenger, 1991). Each person belongs to many communities of practice but with varying degrees of centrality. In some communities of practice we are only peripherally involved; in others we are centrally involved.

Take an alumni association as an example. Such an association has a formal aspect: It is duly constituted, has rules, has people who administer those rules, has a charter, and so forth. As a community of practice, the alumni association is seen through its activities, those practices that its members engage in together, such as publishing a newsletter, organizing trips, and fund-raising. Your involvement in this community may be quite peripheral: You make an annual contribution and allow your bio to be listed in the magazine. Or your involvement in the community may be more central: You are a committee chairperson who worries whether this year's fund-raising goal will be met. In a community of practice, people closer to the center naturally participate more fully in creating, nurturing, and evolving the meanings of the community. That is, people nearer the center are more involved in the process of leadership than people relatively distant from the center. Being closer to the center may also involve a person in being granted authority: You are given the authority to decide how much money to allocate to certain activities and to hire and fire staff people. This involves you in participating in the leadership process as a person with authority. People in positions of authority often participate in the leadership process in ways different from people with less or no authority and in ways different from people who are farther away from the center of the community of practice for other reasons.

Proximity to the center is not, however, measured only in terms of time spent or position occupied. Also important is the idea of becoming expert in whatever it is that the community practices. Thus, a newly appointed committee chairperson may be relatively distant from the center until learning the ropes and becoming expert in practice through practice. He or she may have some authority (even a great deal of authority) yet that person's participation in the process of leadership will be affected by a less-expert status, which decreases one's centrality in the community. One way to think of proximity is to say that people close to the center of the community are old-timers and those at the periphery are newcomers (Lave & Wenger, 1991). Newcomers with authority and old-timers with authority will likely participate differently in the leadership process (and old-timers without authority will participate in yet another way).

In a healthy community of practice, old-timers—or masters in the practice—allow newcomers to engage in what Lave and Wenger (1991) have termed "legitimate peripheral participation." By allowing newcomers to participate legitimately, though they are not yet expert, old-timers bring the newcomers closer to the center. This learning process is closely akin to the leadership process that creates, nurtures, and evolves the frameworks within which the community understands itself and its relation to the world. An important note here is that the membership with respect to old-timers and newcomers changes over time, with newcomers becoming old-timers and displacing existing old-timers. This process of displacement in a community of practice must play some central role in the evolution of the leadership process; it is presently known as *career planning* or *succession planning* in organizations, and it is viewed as being only marginally related to questions of leadership.

What is the relationship between communities of practice and what we know as hierarchical organizations (or as Jaques [1976] has termed them, "accountability hierarchies")? Such an organization, if it is large and complex, consists of many interconnected and overlapping communities of practice. If we look into organizations for groups of people doing something together and, as a result, sharing common values, beliefs, and attitudes, we might find people engaged in activities such as process engineering, or designing sales campaigns, or working on accounts receivable. This is the operational level of activity. Is there a community of practice at higher levels of organization? Is there a community of practice we could call *manufacturing*, or *sales*, or *finance?* The members of such communities of practice would be those people who manage the various clusters of activity that comprise the operation, and the unifying activity would be administration and management of operational work. At the next higher level of organization (divisional), the community of practice would revolve around people who administer the relations among the functions. Finally, at the executive (corporate) level of the organization, the community of practice would revolve around direction setting and other large-scale orienting activities.

This way of analyzing the various levels in an organization by reference to communities of practice is perhaps not much different from many other ways of looking at organizations (Jaques, 1976; Mintzberg, 1979). It does, however, raise the question of whether there is in any sense a corporate community of practice that includes, for example, both the CEO and the process engineer. In what sense could we say that the process engineer and the CEO are united in a common practice? They are certainly not doing the same thing, and more, they are doing different things in almost complete isolation from each other. If leadership is meaning-making in a community of practice, can leadership occur between the CEO and the process engineer?

Meaning and community are co-constructive. They make each other. It's like the print by Escher in which the right hand is drawing the left hand which is drawing the right hand. Meaning constructs community which constructs meaning. We might call this reflexive process *culture.* In the view we are offering, leadership as an offspring of culture is the meaning-making aspect of culture centered around practice—people doing things together.

Communities of practice embed people in commitments—in allowing others to make claims on them (Farley, 1986). This implies some degree of opening up of individual boundaries, of allowing the concerns, hopes, beliefs, convictions, fears, and destinies of others to become a part of one's own individuality. This in turn implies that leadership is intimately connected to processes of group, community, nation-state, and even species-wide integration and togetherness and ultimately to communal survival, growth, and enhancement. Leadership is uniquely human; it is a key component, perhaps the key component, in our survival strategy.

People in Positions of Authority: A New View of Five Concepts

We are now better able to say what we mean when we talk about leadership as if it were meaning-making in a community of practice. We refer to leadership as a social meaning-making process that takes place as a result of activity or work in a group, instead of referring to leadership as a social-influence process in which individuals get others to engage in activity or work. We mean leadership as the process of connecting people to one another and to some social activity, work, enterprise. We mean leadership as that subspecies of culture-building that arises in communities of practice. We speak of leadership as flowing from meaning instead of meaning as flowing from leadership. We refer to leadership as that which creates commitments in communities of practice. We view leadership as that which connects people to work and to one another at work. We refer to leadership as a social process in which everyone in the community participates.

There are two important areas of leadership that look very different from this new perspective. One, which we hope to devote more time to soon and to report on at some later date, is people with no, or with relatively little, authority. Work in this area is, we believe, vitally important to understanding leadership. Fortunately, Heifetz (in press) has already begun the work, and anyone interested in this topic should read his book.

The other area is people in positions of authority in an accountability hierarchy. Looking at this area of leadership from the meaning-making perspective can make it possible for us to gain a new understanding of such concepts as influence, individual action, motivation, the relationship between authority and leadership, and accountability. Let's look at each of these as we shift from the predominant view of leadership as dominance-cum-social-influence to the view of leadership as social meaning-making.

From Social Influence to Social Meaning-making

With the shift to seeing meaning-making as the basis of leadership, influence is no longer considered the essence of leadership; it becomes, rather, an outcome of leadership. Instead of being seen as an ability that the would-be leader must acquire, or as a commodity that he or she must have in plentiful supply before acts of leadership are attempted, influence is seen as a beneficial outcome of an effective process of leadership. Influence arises as people in the community of practice make commitments to one another and thus allow others to make claims on them.

This shift can thus lead people in positions of authority to view the effectiveness of the leadership process less in terms of how much influence they are personally generating and more in terms of the level of feelings of significance experienced by people in the community. The criterion of effectiveness will be less about how closely the group of followers adheres to a vision or plan, and will look more to the involvement of community members in increasingly central ways—the movement of people from relatively less important, marginal roles toward more important, more central roles; in other words, the criterion will tend to be the rate of increase of significance.

The shift from influence toward meaning-making implies a related shift in how we will view the role of the individual in leadership.

From a Dominant Individual Leader Acting on Followers to People Participating in a Shared Process

With this shift in point of view toward leadership, people in positions of authority will begin to question the paradigm that leadership (whether as an individual act or as a social process) arises in the action of a dominant leader. This is a shift away from understanding leadership as being about what a leader does to understanding it as being something people do together.

The concept, just discussed, of influence as the basis of leadership is allied to the view of leadership as an individually oriented process. The shift in viewpoint here involves moving from seeing the individual as the seat of leadership toward a view that the source of leadership lies in meaning-making in which all members of the community participate to some degree or another, including those people in the community, if any, who possess some kind of authority. Although this shift in point of view seems irrevocably to decentralize leadership, this is not the case. To repeat and emphasize this point: Shifting our view of leadership from that of a dominance-inspired influence process to a socially distributed meaning-making process does not necessarily imply that individually oriented leadership processes involving dominance are not possible or effective. As we will see below, even the most authoritarian modes of leadership can be seen as social meaning-making. What this shift in point of view *does* imply is that individual leadership is a special case (as is shared leadership, for that matter) of an underlying social process of making meaning around practice.

One implication of this for people in positions of authority is that, in adopting this view, they will no longer see their position as automatically granting them status as leader and thus as the fountainhead of leadership. They will instead recognize that the underlying meaning-making process constructs their authority and that, depending on the process, this may or may not make them the principal person in the leadership process. In other words, in this view, people called leaders do not so much produce leadership as they are produced by leadership.

What about dominance, you might ask? What about charisma? Isn't it obvious that leadership is often a matter of a powerful individual taking charge of a situation, influencing people, and making things happen? Well, yes, but the process of taking charge can be seen itself in a social context. How so?

At its most basic level, dominance (we will discuss charisma in a moment) can be seen as a psychophysical phenomenon: physical strength, stamina, and speed matched with psychological courage, determination, and ferocity. This is the arena of the hero and the warrior chief. The demands and commandments of the dominant individual backed by strength and the will to use it define the very reality of those subject to the ruler. The experience of the community unfolds within the structure demanded by the dominant individual and is essentially a drama of survival. But it is also a drama in which all members play some role: Dominance, to be effective as a process of leadership, implies a meaning-making structure in which "followers" are reflexively obedient. This is often an extremely effective process of leadership (in crises and combat, to name just two instances) that has obviously had its uses and continues to be useful.

One reason for shifting our view toward a socially distributed meaning-making process is that to sustain highly individually oriented forms of leadership demands constant renewal through demonstrations of the leader's dominance. Although crises and other moments amenable to individual control usually pass before people can begin to question the leader's dominance, the situation is different in sustained settings, where other individuals will inevitably arise to challenge the leader's strength, intelligence, experience, and so forth. In sustained settings, therefore, in which individual leadership is the predominant model (such as most military organizations around the world), more or less stringent rules pertaining to obedience, duty, and the consequences of insurrection are required. Such rules are, of course, in the view being offered here, themselves part and parcel of the underlying meaning-making process out of which individual leaders arise.

What about charisma and charismatic leadership? Dominance is only one feature of charisma. Extraordinary talents for communicating, forming relationships, and getting inside the hearts and minds of others are added to make the charismatic leader (Fromm, 1941). Weber (in Eisenstadt, 1968) understood charisma as an aura of specialness created around a leader by subordinates. This gift of specialness was seen as being granted to leaders who come forward in a time of crisis and offer extraordinary solutions and act as a savior. The followers are therefore attracted to the leader because they feel their own powers derive from those of the leader. This reminds us of Churchill. But did Churchill's charisma arise from within his individuality alone? Or was some larger social context also involved?

Another view of charismatic leadership offered by Edward Shils (1965) points to both the individual component of charisma—the numen, the spirit within—and its social component—the involvement of the charismatic leader at the heart of things, the center, that is, arenas (institutions such as the law, education, and politics) where ideas play out in important ways in people's lives. Thus charisma does not arise only out of an individual's specialness but also out of the individual being deeply involved in the thick of things, either going with or going against main ideas and actions that largely affect people's lives.

The shift toward a social-participation view of leadership allows us to consider that individual leadership may be effective when the leader represents (re-presents, that is, presents in a new way) or allows recognition (re-cognition, that is, knowing in a new way) of that which is inarticulate or unknown yet present in the community of practice. The leader's involvement in the "heart of things" implies profound connectedness to a social whole—else there is no heart to be close to. This view connects the psychological (the individual's knowing) and social (the significance of the knowledge for the community) aspects of charisma. Thus what can be seen as an example of the preeminence of an individual through charismatic leadership can also be seen as a collective process of meaning-making.

An example of this is Queen Elizabeth I. Clifford Geertz (1983) says, "Her whole public life . . . was transformed into a kind of philosophical masque in which everything stood for some vast idea and nothing took place unburdened with parable. . . . Elizabeth ruled a realm in which beliefs were visible, and she but the most conspicuous. . . . The center of the center, Elizabeth not only accepted its transformation of her into a moral idea, she actively cooperated in it. It was out of this—her willingness to stand proxy, not for God, but for the virtues he ordained, and especially for the Protestant version of them—that her charisma grew." (p. 129). It was this participation in a community organized around Protestant virtues and culturally shared ideas of the meaning of royalty that in part granted charismatic qualities to Elizabeth.

Thus, people in positions of authority might be better equipped for their role in the leadership process if they were to become aware of the underlying process of meaning-making by which they gain their authority and are granted their influence. It has individual elements to be sure, but it is also a social phenomenon.

As we move away from viewing leadership as arising necessarily in the individual or as having influence as its basis, we also begin to shift our view with respect to what leadership primarily provides.

From Motivation to Act to Frameworks Within Which to Act

Lying deep beneath the view of leadership as social influence may be the assumption, pointed out by Kelly (1955), that people are essentially inert and require some reason for acting. In other words, we may see leadership as being rooted in influence because we think people need motivating. Instead, we could assume that people are already in motion, already acting, doing, and behaving, and that what they need is not to be prodded but to have some way of guiding their action toward the creation of significance.

In its broadest aspect, motivation, as applied to the question of leadership, has been seen as a more or less dyadic exchange between the person in a position of authority and individuals called *followers*. This exchange has been seen to involve the trading of rewards for performance. The essence of the arrangement is that the person in authority has the resources and power to provide rewards and that the subordinate wants the rewards. Much has been written about the nature of rewards and the nature of people's desire for rewards. Under a view of leadership as social influence, the individual having authority (usually called the *leader*) is seen to be more or less personally responsible for creating motivation to perform. With the shift toward leadership as a social meaning-making process, the understanding of this dynamic changes.

This shift in viewpoint allows people in positions of leadership to see members of the community of action as being already motivated by a desire for increased centrality in the community—increased participation in the more skilled, more knowledgeable aspects of whatever activity the community is organized around. The purpose of the process of leadership in this view is therefore not to create motivation; rather it is to offer legitimate channels for members to act in ways that will increase their feelings of significance and their actual importance to the community. The question, then, for an individual in a position of authority is no longer how to get people to do what is needed but how to participate in a process of structuring the activity and practice of the community so that people marginal to its practice are afforded the means to move toward the center of that practice. In other words, how can the contribution of each person in the community of practice be made increasingly important and increasingly appreciated for its importance?

In discussing this view of leadership, we have thus far been careful not to identify the person in a position of authority as the leader, as is usually done when leadership is viewed as a dominance-cum-social-influence process. The reason for this should become clear in what follows.

From the Authority Figure as De Facto Leader to the Authority Figure as a Participant in a Process of Leadership

In the current view of leadership as a process of social influence, authority and power are associated with leadership by assuming that people in positions of authority and power are leaders. As we have already seen, there is a tendency to see leadership as whatever it is that a leader does; this means that there has been a tendency to see leadership as whatever a person in a position of authority and power does. This tendency has had the effect of making it nearly impossible to think about leadership as a process. Look at a book or article about leadership—even those that aim to discuss leadership as a process—and usually within a page or two, or at most a chapter, the discussion will have centered on individuals called *leaders*. Leadership is seen to flow from the individual in a position of authority toward a group of followers.

When seen as meaning-making, leadership flows around and through a community of practice, interpenetrating the community and including the authority figure (the person, say, with the power to hire and fire members) within its course. The authority figure, in this view, is a participant in the process of leadership who has more power than others in the group. As we will see, a key question arises around the exercise of power and its ultimate implication for the effectiveness of the authority figure's participation in the process of leadership.

Are we saying that directive, authoritarian leadership is not leadership in our terms? Emphatically, no. We contend that even the most directive, unilateral leader can be seen as participating in a shared process of meaning-making in a community of practice. When people in a community accept directive rule from an authority figure, they are participating in the creation of a certain structure of meaning. It may be a structure in which the authority literally tells each person in the community what to do. As long as this is accepted by members of the community, the leadership can be seen as being a shared process in which the participation of the authority figure is defined as acting to direct the activity of all members. Sometimes this may be extremely effective. Almost certainly it is effective in an emergency when there is a single person who knows how to meet the crisis. Its effectiveness becomes questionable in a complex organization engaged in difficult and multifaceted activity. In this latter case, the authority figure will probably need to find some other basis for participation in the process of leadership.

The discussion of our shift in point of view has brought us back to the situation we outlined at the beginning of this paper: What are the key questions a person in a position of authority needs to ask him- or herself? How does the view offered here change these questions?

From "How Do I Take Charge and Make Things Happen?" to "How Do I Participate in an Effective Process of Leadership?"

Seeing leadership from the meaning-making perspective involves forming a new understanding of one's role as a person with authority who is to be held accountable for the performance of others. The traditional approach has been, as suggested, to take charge. Taking charge suggests that authority and power are used to create some variety of influence that gets the job done. In the view of leadership we are offering, because leadership is seen as a process residing in the community of practice (though it is often, not always, embodied in the acts of individuals), the person with authority and power will not so much see his or her role as taking charge as participating. The key movement is from *I* need to make things happen to *we* need to make things happen and *I* need to figure out how best to participate in the process of *us* making things happen.

This shift in viewpoint also requires some reformulation of the relationship between accountability and leadership. Assuming that hierarchies will continue to exist and that individuals in authority roles will continue to be held accountable for the performance of others, we must rethink the nature of individual accountability. The tension for managers in organizations who would participate in leadership rather than be the lone fountainhead of leadership is how to do this while remaining accountable. Yet this tension is not so very different from the tension of being held accountable for tasks that one does not actually perform. The accountable person is deemed to be responsible for assuring that people are well selected, properly trained, and otherwise competent to do the task. So it might be with leadership. The accountable person would be deemed responsible for fostering and nurturing an effective process of leadership and for participating in it effectively.

As we have seen, a key aspect of this shift is the reexamination of the assumption that the only leadership process is one in which influence flows from some authority figure to followers. Our view allows that leadership can happen in other ways. But this is not to say that leadership is never effective when it manifests itself as influence flowing from authority to followers. In times of crisis, for example, when the authority figure is the only person with a sure sense of what to do to steer out of the crisis, a process of leadership in which the authority figure's greater experience and knowledge lead to strong influence of followers will probably be the most effective process. The difference in this situation from this view of leadership is that the underlying process is seen to be meaning-making rather than dominance-cum-influence. The influence in this situation is seen to flow from the way the authority figure's greater experience and knowledge are used to interpret and make sense of a crisis situation. It is this sense-making, more than dominance as such, that is seen as leading to influence.

But what of other situations, such as that described at the beginning of this paper where someone is given the assignment of forming a new unit in the corporation? Is it reasonable to assume that in situations when no one knows what is best or even what is possible to do, that the authority figure should assume that taking charge is most effective? Would it not be more reasonable for the authority to ask, "What is the most effective process of leadership?" Another way to ask this is, "What is the most effective way for this community engaged in this particular practice to make sense of our situation?" This question leads to different considerations than asking, "How can I take charge of this situation?" The question of what is the most effective leadership process leads then to the question, "How can I participate in this process effectively?" Thus the authority is faced with two questions, one of the nature of the leadership process and the other of the nature of his or her participation in the process. The determination of the most effective leadership process is itself, perhaps somewhat paradoxically, also part of the leadership process, as is the determination of the authority's most effective mode of participation. Again, the authority can choose to answer these questions only in his or her own mind and to his or her own satisfaction, or the authority can choose to work through these questions in the community. The criterion will be effectiveness. Which works better? Our guess is that the working through of these questions will be better done in the community and that this will require some level of openness and the ability to create dialogue (Dixon, in press) in the community.

Implications: So What Is Leadership Development?

Leadership development has traditionally been concerned with the individual manager who has authority and is held responsible; it has typically aimed to improve his or her ability to direct and influence others. If leadership is understood as a social meaning-making process, however, our concept of leadership development changes.

We discuss our perspective on leadership development—and what this means for programs—at length in another paper (Palus & Drath, in press). We will only raise a few keys points here.

To begin with, if leadership is seen as meaning-making in a community of practice, then leadership development must involve more than the individual; in fact, it probably should not be primarily concerned with the individual. Instead, it must involve the development (the evolution of ways of being in the world) of the whole community, a process for which each individual takes responsibility. In this view, leadership development is closely related to the process of leadership itself. In fact, it is the renewal of leadership itself.

What does this mean? It means that leadership development can be understood as the evolution in time of the constructions (meaning-making structures) of the community of practice. That is, in terms of a Piagetian (1954) model of how meaning-making develops that has been extended and amplified by others (Basseches, 1984; Kegan, 1982; Kohlberg, 1976), we believe leadership can be thought of as an adaptive process that coordinates and maintains the equilibrium of the community, both within itself and in its relations with the world-at-large. In encountering the world and the inevitable change in the world and within itself, any given structure for making sense of things will come up against things that do not work, do not make sense, cannot be handled, and so forth. This creates an imbalance or incapacity that challenges the adaptive sense-making process to correct itself. It is at this point that the leadership process begins to develop, to evolve toward more adaptive meaning-making that can assimilate or accommodate to the changed conditions. In communities of practice this happens when individual members develop psychologically, when new forms of practice are created, when new ways of bringing people within the community into relationship with one another (structuring the organization) evolve along with ways of relating the community to the world at large.

Individual members may develop psychologically when they evolve more comprehensive ways of seeing themselves and their place in the world. A thorough exposition of what this means can be found in *The Evolving Self: Problem and Process in Human Development* by Robert Kegan (1982). In essence, individual development can be seen as the gradual creation of a capacity for understanding oneself simultaneously in terms of one's unique individuality and as a being deeply embedded in some social surround—in Kegan's terms, understanding oneself as an embedual as well as an individual. As the capacity to hold these two seemingly opposed ideas of self develops, so the person develops the capacity for acting in more flexible and adaptive ways. Thus, by viewing leadership as a social meaning-making process, we are able to see the connections between leadership development and individual psychological development.

Leadership also develops (that is, the process of meaning-making in the community of practice develops) when the forms of practice develop. As organizations strive to get closer to customers, for example, and as this brings about changes in what people do on a day-to-day basis in the community, leadership develops; it evolves toward processes more fit and effective for making sense of the evolving practice. Leadership processes may evolve toward being more individually oriented or toward being more distributed, depending on how practice evolves. However this may happen, a key problem in leadership development is recognizing those elements of the community in which we are embedded that may need revision and reevaluation if leadership is to continue to be effective.

Finally, leadership develops when people as people are brought into new ways of relating to others in the community of practice. These new ways of relating will often be connected to changes in the practice itself. As many organizations today experiment with various forms of meetings that encourage greater openness and dialogue as a vehicle for organizational learning, the process of leadership in these organizations is developing. Little wonder that some people in authority are looking about and scratching their heads, wondering what are their jobs now. To the extent that they see their role as taking charge and making things happen (the traditional approach to leadership), they may see an increasingly marginal role for themselves; but to the extent that they can understand themselves as participants in an evolving process of meaning-making, they will be able to ask themselves questions, like the ones we raised in our introduction, about the most effective process and their most effective means of participating in that process.

So what about traditional leadership development? Should we abandon individual training in leadership? We think not. There is, however, an important difference in the kind of training we pursue. If, in the past, leaders have been trained to exercise leadership, they will now be trained to participate in leadership. This is something like the difference between training an athlete in the individual skills of a sport and training that athlete in the team skills of the sport. Usually the individual skills are learned first. So it may be with leadership. Young supervisors and managers may need to learn the individual skills of leadership and later, as they approach higher levels of management, learn the community-oriented, meaning-making capacities, such as: (1) the capacity to understand oneself as both an individual and as a socially embedded being; (2) the capacity to understand systems in general as mutually related and interacting and continually changing; (3) the capacity to take the perspective of another; and (4) the capacity to engage in dialogue. We leave it for another time to explore how these capacities might be fostered in today's organizations.

Conclusion: Changing Constructs of Leadership

In presenting this way of looking at leadership—as meaning-making in communities of practice—we are suggesting that leadership is itself a social construct, an artifact of that ever-rolling process of making sense of this world we share. Surely our way of understanding leadership has evolved over time and continues to do so.

We can think about our earliest ways of understanding leadership as arising in dominance. We can take a process-view of dominance as a meaning-making activity. Think of a group of primates ruled by one dominant individual. The process of dominant leadership can be described thus: The most powerful (the strongest, smartest) individual enforces compliance with his or her individual needs and wants; power produces compliance through the linking of fear and protection—the followers are afraid of the dominant individual and therefore feel protected by that individual. This can be summarized, in terms of process, as power producing compliance through fear-cum-protection.

Perhaps, as the means by which dominant individuals exercised their power, such as muscle and wits, became available to more people through technology (weapons and writing, for example), dominance began to need supplementing as a way of constructing (understanding) leadership. What may then have entered into the leadership construct is the possibility of people being persuaded by other people, and we get leadership as an influence process. This construct is likely quite old, by the way. *The Oxford English Dictionary,* based on a use of the word dating to the thirteenth century, defines one sense of the verb *lead* as being "to bring by persuasion into a condition." This is, for all its age, a pretty good summation of many of our current definitions of leadership.

Influence as the basis for understanding leadership can also be understood as a meaning-making process. We might say (somewhat awkwardly because our language is weak in conveying process) that periodic influential inputs from persuasive individuals continuously build and refine people's belief that they are engaged in some beneficial activity. Briefly put, this process can be summarized as persuasiveness producing conviction. This is the essence, perhaps, of the meaning-making process of influence.

The key idea here is that we humans did not and have not replaced the dominance construct with the influence construct. We have more likely supplemented dominance with influence. Influence as a way of understanding leadership is layered over dominance as a way of understanding leadership. This makes our construct richer and more useful, but it also leads to confusion and uncertainty. While one person may point to the need for leaders to bring people to a condition by persuasion, another person may point out that often leaders must act independently and dominate situations for the good of all. We are confused: Is leadership influence or dominance? Is influence just a softer way to practice dominance? How are individual traits related to dominance, such as intelligence and a deep voice, related to the ability to influence others? Isn't leadership, after all, just that which people called leaders do? And thus we search for the key to leadership in the layers of our ways of constructing leadership.

More recently, a new layer, a new way of understanding leadership has been added: *participative leadership,* it might be termed. This layer adds to both the richness and the confusion. How can leaders take charge of a situation and act influentially while still allowing real participation? Isn't participation just a more clever way to gain influence? And isn't it ultimately just a much deeper ploy to gain dominance? And if leaders really do allow participation, doesn't one person finally have to make a decision? And then what happens to participation? Again, we search for the elusive key to leadership among the convoluted layers of our constructs of leadership.

We are suggesting that there is a way of understanding leadership that has the potential for sorting out all the others and getting us past our confusion without giving up richness: leadership as meaning-making or sense-making. Whenever people are doing something together for any period of time extended enough to form a community, we can usefully think of the striving to make things make sense, to create meaning out of that experience, as the process of leadership—however that process plays out and with whatever participation by various individuals.

Our constructs of leadership, it seems, have been built up around what is perhaps, ultimately, an epiphenomenon—the powerful individual taking charge. This aspect of leadership is like the whitecaps on the sea—prominent and captivating, flashing in the sun. But to think about the sea solely in terms of the tops of waves is to miss the far vaster and more profound phenomenon out of which such waves arise—it is to focus attention on the tops and miss the sea beneath. And so leadership may be much more than the dramatic whitecaps of the individual leader, and may be more productively understood as the deep blue water we all swim in when we work together.

Bibliography

Basseches, M. (1984). *Dialectical thinking and adult development.* Norwood, NJ: Ablex.

Bennis, W. (1991, August). Creative Leadership. *Executive Excellence,* pp. 5 - 6.

Berger, P., & Luckman, T. (1966). *The social construction of reality: A treatise in the sociology of knowledge.* New York: Doubleday.

Bruner, J. (1986). *Actual minds, possible worlds.* Cambridge, MA: Harvard University Press.

Dixon, N. (in press). *The organizational learning cycle: How we can learn collectively.* New York: McGraw-Hill.

Eisenstadt, S. N. (1968). *Max Weber on charisma and institution building.* Chicago, IL: University of Chicago.

Farley, M. (1986). *Personal commitments.* San Francisco: Harper & Row

Fingarette, H. (1963). *The self in transformation.* New York: Harper & Row.

Fromm, E. (1941). *Escape from freedom.* New York: Avon.

Geertz, C. (1983). *Local knowledge: Further essays in interpretive anthropology.* New York: Basic Books.

Goodman, N. (1978). *Ways of worldmaking.* Indianapolis: Hackett Publishing.

Goodman, N. (1984). *Of mind and other matters.* Cambridge, MA.: Harvard University Press.

Heifetz, R. (in press). *Leadership without easy answers.* Cambridge, MA: Harvard University Press.

Jaques, E. (1976). *A general theory of bureaucracy.* London, England: Heinemann.

Kegan, R. (1982). *The evolving self: Problem and process in human development.* Cambridge, MA: Harvard University Press.

Kelly, G. A. (1955). *The psychology of personal constructs.* New York: Norton.

Kohlberg. (1976). *Collected papers on moral development and moral education.* Cambridge, MA: Center for Moral Education.

Lave, J., & Wenger, E. (1991). *Situated learning: Legitimate peripheral participation.* Cambridge, England: Cambridge University Press.

Mintzberg, H. (1979). *The structuring of organizations: A synthesis of the research.* Englewood Cliffs, NJ: Prentice-Hall.

Palus, C. J., & Drath, W. H. (in press). *Understanding leadership development: A model for program design.* Greensboro, NC: Center for Creative Leadership.

Perry, W. G. (1968). *Forms of intellectual and ethical development in the college years.* New York: Holt, Rinehart, and Winston.

Piaget, J. (1954). *The construction of reality in the child.* New York: Basic Books.

Pondy, L. R. (1978). Leadership is a language game. In M. W. McCall & M. M. Lombardo (Eds.). *Leadership: Where else can we go?* Durham, NC: Duke University Press.

Schein, E. H. (1992). *Organizational culture and leadership* (2nd ed.). San Francisco: Jossey-Bass.

Shils, E. (1965, April). Charisma, order, and status. *American Sociological Review.*

Smircich, L., & Morgan, G. (1982). Leadership: The management of meaning. *Journal of Applied Behavioral Science. 18,* 257-273.

CENTER FOR CREATIVE LEADERSHIP
New Releases, Best-sellers, Bibliographies, and Special Packages

NEW RELEASES

IDEAS INTO ACTION GUIDEBOOKS
Ongoing Feedback: How to Get It, How to Use It Kirkland & Manoogian (1998, Stock #400) $6.95*
Reaching Your Development Goals McCauley & Martineau (1998, Stock #401) $6.95*
Becoming a More Versatile Learner Dalton (1998, Stock #402) $6.95*
Giving Feedback to Subordinates Buron & McDonald-Mann (1999, Stock #403) $6.95

Choosing Executives: A Research Report on the Peak Selection Simulation Deal, Sessa, & Taylor (1999, Stock #183) $20.00
Coaching for Action: A Report on Long-term Advising in a Program Context Guthrie (1999, Stock #181) $20.00
The Complete Inklings: Columns on Leadership and Creativity Campbell (1999, Stock #343) $30.00
Geographically Dispersed Teams: An Annotated Bibliography (Sessa, Hansen, Prestridge, & Kossler (1999, Stock #346) $20.00
High-Performance Work Organizations: Definitions, Practices, and an Annotated Bibliography Kirkman, Lowe, & Young (1999, Stock #342) $20.00
Internalizing Strengths: An Overlooked Way of Overcoming Weaknesses in Managers Kaplan (1999, Stock #182) $15.00
Positive Turbulence: Developing Climates for Creativity, Innovation, and Renewal Gryskiewicz (1999, Stock #2031) $32.95
Selecting International Executives: A Suggested Framework and Annotated Bibliography London & Sessa (1999, Stock #345) $20.00
Spirit and Leadership Moxley (1999, Stock #2035) $30.95
Workforce Reductions: An Annotated Bibliography Hickok (1999, Stock #344) $20.00

BEST-SELLERS
The Adventures of Team Fantastic: A Practical Guide for Team Leaders and Members Hallam (1996, Stock #172) $20.00
Breaking Free: A Prescription for Personal and Organizational Change Noer (1997, Stock #271) $25.00
Breaking the Glass Ceiling: Can Women Reach the Top of America's Largest Corporations? (Updated Edition) Morrison, White, & Van Velsor (1992, Stock #236A) $13.00
The Center for Creative Leadership Handbook of Leadership Development McCauley, Moxley, & Van Velsor (Eds.) (1998, Stock #201) $65.00*
CEO Selection: A Street-smart Review Hollenbeck (1994, Stock #164) $25.00*
Choosing 360: A Guide to Evaluating Multi-rater Feedback Instruments for Management Development Van Velsor, Leslie, & Fleenor (1997, Stock #334) $15.00*
A Cross-National Comparison of Effective Leadership and Teamwork: Toward a Global Workforce Leslie & Van Velsor (1998, Stock #177) $15.00
Eighty-eight Assignments for Development in Place Lombardo & Eichinger (1989, Stock #136) $15.00*
Enhancing 360-degree Feedback for Senior Executives: How to Maximize the Benefits and Minimize the Risks Kaplan & Palus (1994, Stock #160) $15.00*
Evolving Leaders: A Model for Promoting Leadership Development in Programs Palus & Drath (1995, Stock #165) $15.00*
Executive Selection: A Look at What We Know and What We Need to Know DeVries (1993, Stock #321) $20.00*
Executive Selection: A Research Report on What Works and What Doesn't Sessa, Kaiser, Taylor, & Campbell (1998, Stock #179) $30.00*
Feedback to Managers (3rd Edition) Leslie & Fleenor (1998, Stock #178) $60.00*
Four Essential Ways that Coaching Can Help Executives Witherspoon & White (1997, Stock #175) $10.00
A Glass Ceiling Survey: Benchmarking Barriers and Practices Morrison, Schreiber, & Price (1995, Stock #161) $15.00
High Flyers: Developing the Next Generation of Leaders McCall (1997, Stock #293) $27.95
How to Design an Effective System for Developing Managers and Executives Dalton & Hollenbeck (1996, Stock #158) $15.00*
If I'm In Charge Here, Why Is Everybody Laughing? Campbell (1984, Stock #205) $9.95*

If You Don't Know Where You're Going You'll Probably End Up Somewhere Else Campbell (1974, Stock #203) .... $9.95 *
International Success: Selecting, Developing, and Supporting Expatriate Managers Wilson & Dalton (1998, Stock #180) .... $15.00 *
Leadership Education: A Source Book of Courses and Programs Schwartz, Freeman, & Axtman (Eds.) (1998, Stock #339) .... $40.00 *
Leadership Resources: A Guide to Training and Development Tools Schwartz, Freeman, & Axtman (Eds.) (1998, Stock #340) .... $40.00 *
The Lessons of Experience: How Successful Executives Develop on the Job McCall, Lombardo, & Morrison (1988, Stock #211) $27.50
A Look at Derailment Today: North America and Europe Leslie & Van Velsor (1996, Stock #169) .... $20.00 *
Making Common Sense: Leadership as Meaning-making in a Community of Practice Drath & Palus (1994, Stock #156) .... $15.00 *
Making Diversity Happen: Controversies and Solutions Morrison, Ruderman, & Hughes-James (1993, Stock #320) $20.00
Managerial Promotion: The Dynamics for Men and Women Ruderman, Ohlott, & Kram (1996, Stock #170) $15.00
Managing Across Cultures: A Learning Framework Wilson, Hoppe, & Sayles (1996, Stock #173) $15.00
Maximizing the Value of 360-degree Feedback Tornow, London, & CCL Associates (1998, Stock #295) .... $42.95 *
The New Leaders: Guidelines on Leadership Diversity in America Morrison (1992, Stock #238A) $18.50
Perspectives on Dialogue: Making Talk Developmental for Individuals and Organizations Dixon (1996, Stock #168) .... $20.00 *
Preventing Derailment: What To Do Before It's Too Late Lombardo & Eichinger (1989, Stock #138) $25.00
The Realities of Management Promotion Ruderman & Ohlott (1994, Stock #157) .... $15.00 *
Selected Research on Work Team Diversity Ruderman, Hughes-James, & Jackson (Eds.) (1996, Stock #326) $24.95
Should 360-degree Feedback Be Used Only for Developmental Purposes? Bracken, Dalton, Jako, McCauley, Pollman, with Preface by Hollenbeck (1997, Stock #335) .... $15.00 *
Take the Road to Creativity and Get Off Your Dead End Campbell (1977, Stock #204) .... $9.95 *
Twenty-two Ways to Develop Leadership in Staff Managers Eichinger & Lombardo (1990, Stock #144) $15.00

BIBLIOGRAPHIES

Formal Mentoring Programs in Organizations: An Annotated Bibliography Douglas (1997, Stock #332) $20.00
Management Development through Job Experiences: An Annotated Bibliography McCauley & Brutus (1998, Stock #337) $20.00
Selection at the Top: An Annotated Bibliography Sessa & Campbell (1997, Stock #333) .... $20.00 *
Succession Planning: An Annotated Bibliography Eastman (1995, Stock #324) .... $20.00 *
Using 360-degree Feedback in Organizations: An Annotated Bibliography Fleenor & Prince (1997, Stock #338) .... $15.00 *

SPECIAL PACKAGES

Executive Selection (Stock #710C; includes 157, 164, 179, 180, 321, 333) $85.00
Guidebook Package (Stock #721; includes 400, 401, 402) $14.95
HR Professional's Info Pack (Stock #717C; includes 136, 158, 169, 201, 324, 334, 340) $100.00
Leadership Education and Leadership Resources Package (Stock #722; includes 339, 340) $70.00
New Understanding of Leadership (Stock #718; includes 156, 165, 168) $40.00
Personal Growth, Taking Charge, and Enhancing Creativity (Stock #231; includes 203, 204, 205) ... $20.00
The 360 Collection (Stock #720C; includes 160, 178, 295, 334, 335, 338) $75.00

Discounts are available. Please write for a Resources catalog. Address your request to: Publication, Center for Creative Leadership, P.O. Box 26300, Greensboro, NC 27438-6300, 336-286-4480, or fax to 336-282-3284. Purchase your publications from our on-line bookstore at **www.ccl.org/publications**. All prices subject to change.

*Indicates publication is also part of a package.

ORDER FORM

Or e-mail your order via the Center's on-line bookstore at www.ccl.org

Name _____ Title _____

Organization _____

Mailing Address _____
(street address required for mailing)

City/State/Zip _____

Telephone _____ FAX _____
(telephone number required for UPS mailing)

Quantity	Stock No.	Title	Unit Cost	Amount

CCL's Federal ID Number is 237-07-9591.

Subtotal

Shipping and Handling
(add 6% of subtotal with a $4.00 minimum; add 40% on all international shipping)

NC residents add 6% sales tax; CA residents add 7.75% sales tax; CO residents add 6.1% sales tax

TOTAL

METHOD OF PAYMENT
(ALL orders for less than $100 must be PREPAID.)

❏ Check or money order enclosed (payable to Center for Creative Leadership).

❏ Purchase Order No. _____ (Must be accompanied by this form.)

❏ Charge my order, plus shipping, to my credit card:
　　❏ American Express　❏ Discover　❏ MasterCard　❏ VISA

ACCOUNT NUMBER: _____ EXPIRATION DATE: MO. ____ YR. ____

NAME OF ISSUING BANK: _____

SIGNATURE _____

❏ Please put me on your mailing list.

Publication • Center for Creative Leadership • P.O. Box 26300
Greensboro, NC 27438-6300
336-286-4480 • FAX 336-282-3284

fold here

PLACE STAMP HERE

CENTER FOR CREATIVE LEADERSHIP
PUBLICATION
P.O. Box 26300
Greensboro, NC 27438-6300